A Walk by the Seine
Canadian Poets on Paris

A Walk by the Seine
Canadian Poets on Paris

Edited by Cary Fagan

Black Moss Press

Published by Black Moss Press 2450 Byng Road
Windsor, Ontario N8W 3E8
Black Moss books are published with the assistance of the
Canada Council, the Ontario Arts Council and
the Department of Canadian Heritage.

Black Moss books are distributed by Firefly Books,
250 Sparks Ave., Willowdale, Ontario M2H 2S4.
All orders should be directed there.

Cover painting: Clara Sophia Hagarty, *Flower Market, Paris*, 1900.
Government of Ontario Art Collection, Toronto. Photograph by Tom
Moore Photography. Cover design by Richard Withey.

Canadian Cataloguing in Publication Data:

A walk by the Seine : Canadian poets on Paris

Poems.

ISBN 0-88753-267-5

1. Canadian Poetry (English)—20th century. 2. Paris (France)—Poetry. I. Fagan,
Cary

PS8287.P37W34 1995   CB11' .508'03244361   C95-900510-2
PR9195.85.P27W34 1995

Black Moss Press

ACKNOWLEDGEMENTS

"The Jews of Paris" by J.M. Cameron from *The Music Is in the Sadness*, by permission of The Porcupine's Quill. "To Paul Verlaine" by Bliss Carman from *Bliss Carman's Poems,* McClelland & Stewart, 1931. "Watercolour for Negro Expatriates in France" by George Elliott Clarke from *Lush Dreams, Blue Exile*, by permission of the author. "Paris Is Not a Dream" by Karen Connelly from *This Brighter Prison: A Book of Journeys*, by permission of The Porcupine's Quill. Excerpt from "Dead in France" by Frank Davey from *Popular Narratives* © 1991, by permission of Talon Books Ltd., Vancouver, Canada. "Montparnasse" by Don Domanski from *Wolf-Ladder*, by permission of Coach House Press. "Making It in the City" and "For Joan Miró on His 85th Birthday" by David Donnell from *Settlements*, by permission of the Canadian Publishers, McClelland & Stewart, Toronto. "45," "46," and "47" by Louis Dudek from *Europe*, by permission of The Porcupine's Quill. "Giving," "Couple," and "Radnóti" by Cary Fagan from *The Little Black Dress: Tales from France*, by permission of the author. "Harry's New York Bar in Paris" by Douglas Fetherling from *Selected Poems*, by permission of the author. "Eiffelwise" by Robert Finch from *Dover Beach Revisited and other Poems*, by permission of the author. "Organ-Recital, Notre-Dame-de-Paris" by Robert Finch from *Has and Is*, by permission of The Porcupine's Quill. "At Cafe Le Poêle" and "Riding the Paris Metro" by C.H. Gervais from *Into a Blue Morning*, and "Letter to Jean Cocteau" in *Letters from the Equator*, by permission of the author. Excerpt from "The Day" by John Glassco from *Selected Poems*, © 1971 by Oxford University Press Canada, by permission of Oxford University Press Canada. "At the Rue de Buci One Evening" by Ralph Gustafson from *Tracks in the Snow*, by permisson of the author. "Le Rendezvous des Gourmets" by Darly Hine from *Minutes*, by permission of the author. "Exhibition at the Louvre" by Judith Krause from *Half the Sky*, by permission of Coteau Books. "The Day Aviva Came to Paris" by Irving Layton from *A Wild Peculiar Joy: Selected Poems 1945-82*, by permission of the Canadian Publishers, McClelland & Stewart, Toronto. "Old Trees at Pere La Chaise" and "Doves" by Dorothy Livesay from *Right Hand Left Hand*, by permission of the author. "Apollinaire" by Bruce Meyer from *The Open Room*, by permission of Black Moss Press. "Cocteau" and "Apollinaire" by Stan Persky from *Wrestling the Angel*, by permission of the author. "Parisian Courtyard" by Janet Read from *Blue Mind's Flower*, by permission of Moonstone Press.

"Rue Delambre," "The decade was dead, and everyone," and "To Hell with Paris" (untitled poems) by Stephen Scobie from *McAlmon's Chinese Opera*, by permission of the author. "Metro" by Stephen Scobie from *Ghosts: A Glossary of the Intertext*, by permission of Wolsak and Wynn. "Place de la Concorde" by F.R. Scott from *The Collected Poems of F.R.Scott*, by permisson of the Canadian Publishers, McClelland & Stewart, Toronto. "It Is Later than You Think" by Robert Service from *Ballads of a Bohemian*, © Dutton, by permission of Putnam Publishing Group and the Estate of Robert Service. "Pont Neuf on a Rainy Morning. 1931," "Dancer. Centre Pompidou. 1988"," and "Chairs. Champs-Elysées. 1988" by Steven Ross Smith from *Transient Light*, by permission of the author. "A Walk by the Seine" by Phyllis Webb from *Even Your Right Eye*, by permission of the author. "Jardin du Luxembourg" by Andrew Wreggitt" from *Poetry Canada Review* (volume 14, number 1, 1993), by permission of the author. "I had always sensed Paris" (untitled poem) by Patricia Young from *All I Ever Needed Was a Beautiful Room*, by permission of Oolichan Books.

Introduction Sources

Brown, Russell. "Callaghan, Glassco, and the Canadian Lost Generation." *Essays In Canadian Writing* 51-52 (Winter 1993-Spring 1994): 83-112.

Callaghan, Morley. *That Summer In Paris*. Toronto: Macmillan, 1963.

Carman, Bliss. *Letters of Bliss Carman*. Edited by H. Pearson Gundy. Montreal: McGill-Queens University Press, 1982.

Clarke, George Elliott. "To Paris Burning." *Writing Away: The Pen Canada Travel Anthology*. Edited by Constance Rooke. Toronto: McClelland & Stewart, 1994.

Fagan, Cary. "We'll Always Have Paris." *Books In Canada* May 1989: 2-3.

Glassco, John. *Memoirs of Montparnasse*. Toronto: Oxford University Press, 1970.

Gnarowski, Michael. "Europe—The History as Afterward." *Europe* by Louis Dudek. Erin: Porcupine's Quill, 1991: 147-158.

Klinck, Carl F. *Robert Service*. Toronto: McGraw-Hill Ryerson, 1976.

Kokotailo, Philip. *John Glassco's Richer World:* Memoirs of Montparnasse. Toronto: ECW Press, 1988.

Livesay, Dorothy. *Right Hand Left Hand*. Erin, Ontario: Press Porcépic, 1977.

Meyer, Bruce, and Brian O'Riordan. "A Sense of Wonder: An Interview With Marty Gervais." *Poetry Canada Review* Vol. 14 No. 4 (1994): 1, 3, 29.

Miller, Muriel. *Bliss Carman: Quest and Revolt*. St. John's: Jesperson Press, 1985.

Scobie, Stephen. "Afterword." *McAlmon's Chinese Opera*. Dunvegan, Ontario: Quadrant, 1980: 89-93.

Service, Robert. *The Complete Poems of Robert Service*. New York: Dodd, Mead, 1940.

Stevens, Peter. *Dorothy Livesay: Patterns in a Poetic Life*. Toronto: ECW Press, 1992.

A NOTE ON THE POEMS

The spellings, accents, and capitalizations of French words and names in these poems vary widely. I have made no changes in the texts for the sake of consistency.

In memory of Ralph Gustafson,
great friend and poet

Contents

9

Introduction

The poems gathered here sing with the music in the streets, the noise of Sorbonne students arguing in cafés, the jostle of tourists crowding Notre-Dame cathedral. Anyone who has been to Paris or has just read about it will recognize the Luxembourg Gardens, the dome of Sacré Coeur, the performer in front of the Pompidou.

But above all, these poems conjure a city of artists. As David Donnell writes, "What can you say except that Paris was an age of masters / who wrote and painted under sunnier skies than our own."

*

On April 18, 1896, Bliss Carman sailed for Europe on the Cunard steamship the *S.S. Cephalonia*. Born in Fredericton, Carman was thirty-five years old and had already published several books, although he was struggling to make a living. In Paris, he and an American friend stayed in a small flat in Montmartre. He had introductions to a number of French poets who considered him a North-American version of a Symboliste. Actually, Carman had doubts about both Baudelaire (too depraved) and Mallarmé (too ethereal), but he did feel an affinity with Verlaine, whose melancholy poems Carman had translated.

"Ten days in Paris, and not an idiom unslaughtered when I was through with it," Carman joked afterwards in a letter. Yet he loved Paris in a way that he could not feel about London, which he had also visited. Not long after going home again he heard that Verlaine had died, his last days a trial of poverty and sorrow. Carman, who felt that the public did not sufficiently appreciate his own work, may have feared that his life might end like the French poet's. And so he wrote "To Paul Verlaine." Published in 1898, it is both a feeling elegy and a vivid poem about a city whose beauty makes its indifference to a great son all the more painful.

*

It seems only appropriate that our image of artistic Paris should be, at least in part, a literary creation. Henri Murger, a clerk who gave up respectability to become a writer and painter, started it with his *Scènes de la vie de Bohème*. First published as a magazine serial in the 1840s, it was turned into a play and, most famously, the opera by Puccini. Murger's episodic novel is equally cynical and romantic as young artists

12

inhabit garrets in the Latin Quarter, where they burn manuscripts to keep warm.

Some of the the literary portraits of Bohemian life that followed were more artful. George Moore, a young Irishman who went to Paris wanting to be a painter, published his memoir, *Confessions of a Young Man*, in 1888. One of the many who came to Paris after reading Moore was Robert Service. Service was forty and already famous as the author of such popular verses as "The Shooting of Dan McGrew" when he arrived in Paris in the spring of 1913. He took a garret room on the Quai Voltaire, wandered the city, and began to take art lessons and dress in a broad-brimmed hat and velveteen jacket. He was no poor student or artist, although he liked to pretend otherwise. In later years he would see Gertrude Stein in the street and even meet Henry Miller, but he was suspicious of the modernists and resentful of their pretensions.

Service married a French woman, became an ambulance driver during the Great War, and after the armistice used his increasing income to take a sumptuous apartment on the Place du Panthéon. He began to write a verse and prose sequence in the voice of a struggling poet living in Paris before the war. *Ballads of a Bohemian* was completed in 1919 and published in 1921. In one amusing incident, the poet manages to sell a verse written in the style of "Sourdough" Service himself:

> I don't think much of his stuff, but they say he makes heaps
> of money. I can well believe it, for he drives a Hispano-Suiza in
> the Bois every afternoon. The other night he was with a crowd
> at the Dome Café, a chubby chap who sits in a corner and sel-
> dom speaks. I was disappointed. I thought he was a big, hairy
> man who swore like a trooper and mixed brandy with his beer.
> He only drank Vichy, poor fellow!

During the Second World War Service went to Hollywood, which was turning some of his books into movies. He settled in Monte Carlo on the French Riviera, where he died in 1958.

*

Another Canadian writer who was inspired by George Moore to sail for Paris was John Glassco. Glassco, nicknamed Buffy, would become a poet, translator, and author of erotic fiction, but he was only eighteen when he braved his father's disapproval and dropped out of McGill University to go to Paris in 1928. The young Glassco was eager for the good life and caroused with most of the major expatriate figures of the time, including Robert McAlmon, the abrasive, hard-drinking American writer and publisher whose Contact Editions issued books by Ernest Hemingway and Gertrude Stein.

Glassco's place in the expatriate scene of 1920s Paris was pretty much forgotten until Morley Callaghan published his memoir, *That Summer in Paris,* in 1963. In his book Callaghan told how Glassco and his Montreal friend Graeme Taylor helped him and his wife find an apartment on the rue de la Santé. He made fun of Glassco and hinted at his homosexuality, which Glassco preferred to keep private. Callaghan revealed that Glassco and Taylor were the models for the two young men in one of his best-known short stories, "Now That April's Here," which he wrote because of a bet with McAlmon.

Getting back at Callaghan was one of Glassco's motives for completing own memoir, the first chapter of which he had actually written in Paris. In *Memoirs of Montparnasse* (1970), he describes arriving in the city for the first time:

> It was dark, damp, and snowing slightly, and I suppose the city did not look its best from the train windows, but I had only to think I was now in the city of Baudelaire, Utrillo and Apollinaire to be swept by a joy so strong it verged on nausea. Coming out of the Gare du Nord, however, and standing on the wet dark street with a little wall of trunks around me and a vision of half-a-dozen brightly lit cafés opposite, I had a much different impression—the warm, prosy, comfortable feeling of having somehow come home.

In the book, Glassco mentions writing a "sonnet to Paris" in 1928, which was then published in a literary journal. In fact (as Philip Kokotailo has shown in his study, *John Glassco's Richer World*), the sonnet did not appear at the time. It wasn't published for thirty years, and then as a stanza in a long poem called "The Day."

Glassco (or so I believe) made a mistake in burying the sonnet in an otherwise unremarkable poem. Inspired by Arthur Symon's translation of Baudelaire's *Les fleurs du mal,* the sonnet is a fine mood piece in the Decadent mode. It is published here alone for the first time.

*

It was from *Memoirs of Montparnasse* that Stephen Scobie first learned about Robert McAlmon. In 1980 he published *McAlmon's Chinese Opera*, a documentary poem in McAlmon's bitter voice that focussed on his Paris years. Other Canadian poets have also felt an irresistible urge to recreate the lives of artists in Paris—sometimes the same artists, though with very different results. A reader might compare Stan Persky's exuberant prose poems on Cocteau and Apollinaire to poems by C.H. Gervais and Bruce Meyer on the same subjects.

Patricia Young has also written a documentary poem, on the writer Jean Rhys. A frankly autobiographical writer, Rhys' novel *Quartet* is a portrait of her time in 1920s Paris and her involvement in a love triangle with Ford Madox Ford and his wife. As a feminist poet Young believes Rhys to have been emotionally and physically exploited; carefree Paris has its dark side. Yet even for Rhys, Paris was a place where she could sense her real self.

*

Long before Young began imagining the life of Jean Rhys, another Canadian woman poet was trying to find herself in Paris. Dorothy Livesay was twenty-one when she crossed the Atlantic in 1931 for post-graduate studies at the Sorbonne. She had already published a book of poems, but as a woman had felt isolated on the University of Toronto campus. In Paris she declared herself found and wrote to a friend that the city was "lovely":

> ...with perfect weather and the Seine making Paris seem like a dream city because of its bridges and the constant flutter of leaves upon it. And everyone stopping to smell the air, walking among the high trees in the Tuileries to forget the nervous whistle and screech of Paris traffic. And I too walking along peering at bookstalls along the quais; or art exhibitions in the Rue de Seine.

Yet in the same letter Livesay wrote that Europe was in "one hell of a mess. I don't see any way out but the death and burial of Capitalism." In Paris she wrote her first political poems, attended meetings, and began a troubled affair with a man who was also a student from Canada. She would say later that the year in Paris was a watershed in her life.

*

15

Few Canadian poets have stayed in Paris for long, instead treating the city as a site of pilgrimage. (It seems unnecessary to state that I mean *English* Canadian poets. The relation of Quebec writers to Paris is naturally different and undoubtedly more complicated.) Perhaps that is why the romance rarely wears off. Yet there is the occasional poet who takes it as his or her task to expose the "real" Paris to those of us who have been blinded by the brilliance of its charms.

Louis Dudek travelled to the continent in 1953, when he was an instructor at McGill University and the author of two slim volumes of poems. His long poem *Europe* is a bitter lament for a fallen culture, although even he cannot resist a lyric about lovers walking in the night. It is interesting to read his poem on the Place de la Concorde alongside one by F.R. Scott; the difference is a result of temperament as much as historical reading.

The young poet Karen Connelly went to Paris some 40 years after Dudek, but her poem is no less bitter, although it is much more personal. "Paris is not a dream / but a lie," she insists and the city she depicts is luridly lit. But the most devastating poem, and one likely to leave its reader silent in the wake of its mournful and incantatory rhythm, is "The Jews of Paris" by J.M. Cameron.

*

Writers find the tradition they need to nourish their own work, and the literary history of Paris is a rich source from which to draw. In the Paris Metro, C.H. Gervais imagines that he spots Henry Miller, a writer who (as he once noted in an interview) inspired his own desire to write. Frank Davey wanders the Pére-Lachaise cemetery where Gertrude Stein and Jim Morrison are buried. His thoughts of these famous dead mingle with the news that his friend Barrie (the poet bpNichol, an important supporter and example for so many Canadian writers) has died.

George Elliott Clarke grew up in the Black community of Nova Scotia and by his reading became aware of the Black American artists—from Josephine Baker to James Baldwin—who went into exile in Paris to escape the racism of their native country. As he once wrote in a memoir, "Black art seduced me into loving Paris."

*

As a boy I visited Paris with my parents a couple of times. But as a young man I could remember almost nothing of those trips, perhaps

16

because I wanted to discover Paris for myself, as if I had never been there. And so I mark my first real stay to 1976, when I was fresh out of high school. My brother and I went to Paris for a month to study French. We took one look at the school, a concrete pillbox scrawled over with Marxist graffiti, and decided to skip the lessons. It was the summer of the greatest heat wave in recorded European history and we sweated through the streets and museums, keeping pretty much to ourselves and talking about Plato and Machiavelli—books my brother had read in university. In the Bois de Boulogne I picked up a stone, which I wrote about in an early poem; it rests on the desk beside me as I write this.

The last time I visited Paris was in January, 1991. The tourists were staying away, fearing terrorist acts if a Gulf war should break out. The city was cold and breathtakingly beautiful. My wife and I kept warm in cafés, spent whole days in the Louvre, read Baudelaire and Flaubert. One night in a restaurant the owner suddenly turned up the radio; Mitterrand was making a speech of support for the French soldiers. "Vivre La France," he declaimed and I felt as if I'd been sent back in time. But then, at least for pilgrims, Paris will always exist in the past at least as vividly as it does in the present.

*

This modest anthology will hardly change the course of literary studies. It will not redress the grievances of any neglected group. The only genuine reason for its existence is the pleasure that I have had in compiling it and the pleasure that I hope you will experience while reading it. But then we sometimes forget that the purpose of reading poetry is pleasure, with all the complex shadings of that word.

I don't know when I will next return to Paris, but when I do I will bring this book with me. I will stand in the rue de Buci and read aloud Ralph Gustafson, linger by the Seine and recite Phyllis Webb. I will open this book at a little table and for a moment all these poets will be gathered together in the same café. Celebrating, condemning, inventing Paris.

The Dusk Was Lovely

Ralph Gustafson

At the Rue de Buci One Evening

The evening was lovely, the dusk was lovely, the air
Was lovely. Again it was Paris—where they shortchange
Buyers and as a bonus are right. But lovely the crowd,
The people, all of them, thievery elegantly done.
We ran into the noise on the left bank,
On the rue de Buci, music, loved, the rhythm
Smart as heaven, nine of them, trumpet, cornet,
Trombone, two of each, one for the tuba
Broadside, the clarinet between,
O what a group sophisticated—eight of them
With him out front, bass drum, cymbal, pounded
Like crazy, punctual as fate, the girl with the cornet
Zipping the clarinet's zipper at every break,
Gendarmes shouting to let the automobile through.
O it was glory, independence, impregnable joy!

Bliss Carman

To Paul Verlaine

So they would raise your monument,
Old vagabond of lovely earth?
Another answer without words
To Humdrum's, "What are poets worth?"

Not much we gave you when alive,
Whom now we lavishly deplore,—
A little bread, a little wine,
A little caporal—no more.

Here in our lodging of a day
You roistered till we were appalled;
Departing, in your room we found
A string of golden verses scrawled.

The princely manor-house of art,
A vagrant artist entertains;
And when he gets him to the road,
Behold, a princely gift remains.

Abashed, we set your name above
The purse-full patrons of our board;
Remind newcomers with a nudge,
"Verlaine took once what we afford!"

The gardens of the Luxembourg,
Spreading beneath the brilliant sun,
Shall be your haunt of leisure now
When all your wander years are done.

There you shall stand, the very mien
You wore in Paris streets of old,
And ponder what a thing is life,
Or watch the chestnut blooms unfold.

There you will find, I dare surmise,
Another tolerance than ours,
The loving-kindness of the grass,
The tender patience of the flowers.

And every year, when May returns
To bring the golden age again,
And hope comes back with poetry
In your loved land across the Seine,

Some youth will come with foreign speech,
Bearing his dream from over sea,
A lover of your flawless craft,
Apprenticed to your poverty.
He will be mute before you there,
And mark those lineaments which tell
What stormy unrelenting fate
Had one who served his art so well.

And there be yours, the livelong day,
Beyond the mordant reach of pain,
The little gospel of the leaves,
The *Nunc dimittis* of the rain!

Phyllis Webb

A Walk by the Seine

This water flowing
down through a clutch of stones,
this bank we walk along,
and old river-men fishing
toss song in a net of motion
that draws our joined hands
too close to the edge.

This river towing
barges, suicides, small fish, its own
miraculous currents, and the strong
cities of peace and war, all washing
down to an ominous ocean
where even our looping thoughts are fanned
across a sea of knowledge.

These leaning, bearded, dark men knowing
ultimate tragedy moans
like a siren down from the long
sky, cover their eyes, wishing,
wishing they had not seen our devotion
to the straight course in a crooked land
and our final pledge.

But you and I slowing
our words to a muted tone
(for beauty silences the horse-drawn
carriages of wisdom), meshing
light and leaves in that imperial notion
of stasis and dream, move and stand,
like love and death, at the river's edge.

C.H. Gervais

At Cafe Le Poêle

Stanley is a male prostitute.
He learns there is a man
from Houston in Paris
tonight looking
for him. Last night this
man found a jazz bar
where he paid out 15 francs
for the show, but before he
escaped had squandered more than
1,800 francs—for that fare
he was treated to a punkish boy
with a multi-coloured Iroquois cut,
chains, leather, & permitted
the words "Bizarre! Bizarre!"
to be spray-painted up & down
his black silk pant legs. In the
morning when the Texan woke
at the hotel, there were tubes
of Preparation H scattered on
newspapers & the bureau. That is
desperation. The man should
have met Stanley for a more
discreet encounter. Stanley is
cultured, wears cravats, drinks
good wines, carries a briefcase
& writes letters home weekly
to his mother in Medicine Hat.
Stanley is slim & the backs of
his legs are as hard as iron
railings & his hair is flaxen
blonde. Stanley is a giver & a
taker. For him sex is all
bliss & charisma. The bizarre

is translated into the natural
& pleasurable. There are no spankings,
no cigarette burns, no degradation,
only the honey of experience. Tonight
Stanley is having dinner at Cafe
Le Poêle with his sister while he
waits for the Texan. The man
should arrive momentarily. This is
poetry–this moment just before
the rendezvous. Stanley is fully
aware that his presence will please
the man just as the first sight
of hawthorn along the Seine
charms the tourists at the
beginning of Spring.

Riding the Paris Metro

The woman's eyes are chocolate.
Her knees bump against mine
on the Metro. One finger
is bandaged. She is
saintly & the woman next
to her shifts so her knees also
touch mine. My legs are
sandwiched. I am in love.
At the back of the car
two young blonde women strum
guitars & sing *Blowin' in the Wind.*
Soon one approaches with a
cup to collect & I am the only
one to contribute. I get off
at the next stop & there
is someone seated among
scattered Metro tags. He plays
a violin & the wheels of the cars
sing in harmony as they pull away.
Another car arrives. I am sitting
on a bench. A saxophone blares
among faces. I can't see the musician.
Someone resembling Henry Miller
is seated in another car. He is
reading Le Monde. Glasses round,
wire rimmed. I imagine him
leaving cobblestone Villa Seurat
en route to proof read at the old
Chicago Tribune offices. A
black woman is absorbed in his
brilliant tie that drapes outside
his trench coat. She'll follow it
anywhere but he is lost in
the French elections at the end
of the 20th century. A young man

returned to Paris to see
the changes. No one is forgotten
here. Plaques cover buildings
like graffiti. Births & deaths
are the moments marked by historians,
& tourists carry scarlet arrondissement
handbooks to lose themselves in
spaghetti-like streets that wind
into confusion & surprises.
But there is no memory of Miller
here, that French poet Blaise Cendrars
popped in one afternoon to pay
homage. Another Metro car arrives.
A man grasps the silver rail
in the yellow haze of the nearly empty
compartment. His head is bandaged—
Apollinaire! Only one stop away
from St. Germain des Près. Moments
away from his death at 22 Rue St. Germain.
The darkened quarters alive with
eyes of friends—Cocteau &
Picasso & Apollinaire's head
on the pillow like the young Virgil.
There he is this morning—
smiling, reaching into the coat
pocket of his jacket for a small
notebook. The star-shaped drawings!
The Eiffel Tower exploding in
letters revealed in a flash
as the pages flutter open
after the doors shut & the car jerks
away. Apollinaire gone. There is
silence. Only for an instant
till spidery notes of a clarinet
bounce from the opposite platform
& I make out the man playing it.
A kind of jazz eulogy to the dead.
The Metro is deeper than their graves

& its history as continuous. Someone
joins in with a guitar & the jazz
erupts into blues & a black man
with leather pants & white running shoes
begins to dance in slow motion. Another
car arrives. Silver handles turn
& out steps lanky shy Ray Knister.
It is barely the Roaring Twenties
& he is here to blend into
the fabric of the age. He moves
cautiously. Poems of southern
Ontario filter from his eyes. Lake
St. Clair & the mark of his death in
the solitary moment. A steady
tapping interrupts. A blind boy
with a white cane seated on
a nearby bench raps out a staccato
tune for Metro passengers on the platform.
He isn't quick enough to push his way
past everyone to the next car
where there is a woman with
gorgeous white tights, legs crossed
& reading an Iris Murdoch mystery
in English. He asks me to describe her
& I do in my best French & he tells me
in his best English that he waits
for this moment daily & each day
she arrives on the same train.
I am looking for an ending to
all this & see it. Near me is
the brash Cocteau smoking opium
& letting his mind drift to young men
at typewriters & in showers. His hands
tremble with poems & drawings. Drama
lines his face. The two of us leave
on the next train. Together.

Letter to Jean Cocteau

I saw your right hand at Musée Grevin, the wax museum on Blvd.
Montmartre...Those pale, sad, effete, warm fingers. Your writing hand
under the glass case. Lying there like a rubber glove in a white sink. I
fancied concealing it under my raincoat this morning. Taking it away
to a café...Letting it madly compose poems. Permitting it to search my
pockets, autograph my thighs. And all the while I would sip chocolate
chaud & fold & refold the Sunday Telegram, nod obligingly to
hustling waiters... All the while I would try to master that fine balance
your hands affected between art and severance.

David Donnell

Making It in the City

for Barry Callaghan

Picasso lived for years on bread and ideas and bulls
and sold his drawings to friends. After he became famous
the gallery was besieged with thousands of buyers.
His social life improved. Clothing designers pursued him
all over Pigalle to give him expensive boat-neck sweaters.
Women threw themselves at his feet from behind closed doors.
Paris was open. Picasso's greatest early drawings
were of young boys leading horses out of blue space
and beatific couples making love in haystacks.

None of the women I know are throwing themselves at my feet
and the price of art materials makes supper impossible.
Only the pigeons outside Osgoode Hall believe in my kindness.
I wear the torn jacket and the white straw hat.
The blonde girl reading a novel thinks I'm a bum on welfare.
A breeze rustles her skirt, the pigeons lift, the streetcars
rumble by an old friend's bookstore and disappear in traffic.

I get in a cab with some Jamaicans and drive to the racetrack.
The evening races seem like a natural.
My form is marked up with a blueprint analysis of the fifth
and I have a tip from one of the trainers.
Franz Marc is on the other side of the Mutuals window
reading a French newspaper and smoking a short cigar.
He punches my rent money to win and smiles like a magistrate.
My horse gallops home at 99-1 and the track goes dark
except for the electric tote-board and the end of Marc's cigar.
I stand confused in the evening crowd
while several women throw their clothes in the air
and some pink underwear lands in my face.
I pocket the silk and listen for the announcer's voice.
It sounds like Mayakovsky and the saint says my horse is gone
'running in the milky dark beyond the wire'
across all fences into the blue and permanent fields of time.

For Joan Miró on His 85th Birthday

Born in 1893, in Catalonia, province of sunny skies and cool
                                    brown earth,
12 years after Picasso,
                        master of yellow flowers and bizarre
                        red birds,
what can you tell us about the blue skies over spain,
the students sitting around in the cafés of Paris,
the death of Lorca,
                the exile of Buñuel
or the farouche master's new film—*That Obscure Object of Desire?*

What can you say except that Paris was an age of masters
who wrote and painted under sunnier skies than our own.

You are one of the great flowers, one of the great wry birds,
that leap from the human heart
                                like dark speech from the throat
of a young man startled suddenly on a trestle bridge by a horse.

We have the sun and the earth, our mathematics and a good cellar,
but you are a part of the light itself; even the ink-stains on the
print-table in your atelier are inhabited by the birds of the air.

A blind man sees nothing, muses, like the incredible Borges,
or plays hot funk piano with the exuberance of Ray Charles.

Strike us, master, we are the brilliant young men of the grey city,

leave us restless with yellow flowers caught in our shirts
your great birds swooping down to perch on our heads like
                    statues.

Judith Krause

Exhibition at the Louvre

In the sculpture court, I couldn't quite hear
what the couple ahead of me was saying,
their heads bent forward, hat brims almost touching,
shoulders tight against each other's,
but I guessed it might be love,
the words soft as dust
in the clear sunlight.
Knew from the way his hand sought out hers,
the way her pale fingers took his
they shared some small sorrow,
the pain giving them a sombre air,
survivors, in dark winter coats,
the pink-veined marble of the sphinx still
warm several minutes after they leave.

Robert Service

It Is Later than You Think

Lone amid the café's cheer,
Sad of heart am I to-night;
Dolefully I drink my beer,
But no single line I write.
There's the wretched rent to pay,
Yet I glower at pen and ink:
Oh, inspire me, Muse, I pray,
It is later than you think!

Hello! there's a pregnant phrase.
Bravo! let me write it down;
Hold it with a hopeful gaze,
Gauge it with a fretful frown;
Tune it to my lyric lyre...
Ah! upon starvation's brink,
How the words are dark and dire:
It is later than you think.

Weigh them well....Behold yon band,
Students drinking by the door,
Madly merry, *bock* in hand,
Saucers stacked to mark their score.
Get you gone, you jolly scamps;
Let your parting glasses clink;
Seek your long neglected lamps;
It is later than you think.

Look again: yon dainty blonde
All allure and golden grace,
Oh so willing to respond
Should you turn a smiling face.
Play your part, poor pretty doll;
Feast and frolic, pose and prink;

There's the Morgue to end it all,
And it's later than you think.

Yon's a playwright—mark his face,
Puffed and purple, tense and tired;
Pasha-like he holds his place,
Hated, envied and admired.
How you gobble life, my friend;
Wine, and woman soft and pink!
Well, each tether has its end:
Sir, it's later than you think.

See yon living scarecrow pass
With a wild and wolfish stare
At each empty absinthe glass,
As if he saw Heaven there.
Poor damned wretch, to end your pain
There is still the Greater Drink.
Yonder waits the sanguine Seine...
It is later than you think.

Lastly, you who read; aye, you
Who this very line may scan:
Think of all you planned to do...
Have you done the best you can?
See! the tavern lights are low;
Black's the night, and how you shrink!
God! and is it time to go?
Ah! the clock is always slow;
It is later than you think;
Sadly later than you think;
Far, far later than you think.

Up from the Lamplit River

John Glassco

[Sonnet to Paris]

from "The Day"

My soul, recall those midnights in September
When the sleepy autumn winds blew, warm and amorous,
Up from the lamplit river and over us,
Thou and I—whom we must at times remember!
When walking through the night we beheld in visions
Of the sleeping city our spirit's firm repose,
Luxurious, perfect, like those flowers that close
On the bees they have first made drunken with fabulous visions—
Thou who keep'st yet the divine stain of my tears
Psyche, not subject to the enervate years,
Canst though alone now escape those terrible guardians
To roam again that ecstatic city of delights,
Madder than those who pass her superb nights
Dancing to the insane music of her accordions?

Stephen Scobie

Untitled

Rue Delambre
Rue du Montparnasse
Rue Campagne Première

Rue Notre Dame des Champs
Rue du Cardinal Lemoine
Rue de Fleurus

Rue de Vaugirard
Rue du Cherche Midi
Rue Rousselet

Rue Broca
Rue de la Gaîté
Passage d'Enfer

Rue de l'Arrivée
Rue du Départ

(Editor's note: this poem and the following two are written in the voice of Robert McAlmon, American expatriate writer and publisher.)

Untitled

The decade was dead, and everyone
knew it except for the two
susceptible boys. For Glassco and Taylor
everything was new again: the first
night at the Falstaff, the actual thrill
of meeting James Joyce, or even
parading off to Gertrude Stein's.
They were as fresh as flowers of April
blooming in early September.

For Buffy, to be cynical was one
of the social graces: I envied the ease
of disillusion worn like a coat
with impeccable taste. Yet he was open,
naive as a child, susceptible,
spending his body like a man
might spend his money who felt ill at ease
at being rich when all his friends were poor.

Was I ever as young as he was? Could
I ever have acted like him, that night
out of jealous boredom I attacked Kay Boyle
ripping her silly illusions to threads
for all the bar to hear, and she threw
a beer glass at me, which missed
but drenched young Glassco, and he dropped
his head to the counter and cried?

Untitled

To hell with Paris,
with its buildings that don't give a damn
for the people who happen to be there
this particular century,
its buildings impassive as stone
its streets that gather the years
its river that runs through your mind like time—

to hell with Paris,
the city of light be damned,
implacable, relentless, forgiving
nothing from all your wasted days,
I've had enough

of its inescapable
inhuman unbearable
eternal

beauty

Irving Layton

The Day Aviva Came to Paris

The day you came naked to Paris
The tourists returned home without their guidebooks,
The hunger in their cameras finally appeased.

Alone once more with their gargoyles, the Frenchmen
Marvelled at the imagination that had produced them
And once again invited terror into their *apéritifs*.
Death was no longer exiled to the cemeteries.

In their royal gardens where the fish die of old age,
They perused something else besides newspapers
—A volume perhaps by one of their famous writers.
They opened their hearts to let your tender smile defrost them;
Their livers filled with an unassuageable love of justice.
They became the atmosphere around them.

They learned to take money from Americans
Without a feeling of revulsion towards them;
And to think of themselves
As not excessively subtle or witty.
"*Au diable* with Voltaire," they muttered,
"Who was a national calamity.
Au diable with *la République*.
(A race of incurable *petit bourgeois*, the French
Are happiest under a horse under a man.)
Au diable with *la Monarchie!*
We saw no goddesses during either folly;
Our bald-headed savants never had told us
Such a blaze of pubic hair anywhere existed."
And they ordered the grandson of Grandma Moses
To paint it large on the dome of le Sacré Coeur.

My little one, as if under those painted skies

It was again 1848,
They leaped as one mad colossal Frenchman from their café Pernods
Shouting, "*Vive L'Australienne!*
Vive Layton who brought her among us!
Let us erect monuments of black porphyry to them!
Let us bury them in the Panthéon!"
(*Pas si vite, messieurs;* we are still alive.)

And when, an undraped Jewish Venus,
You pointed to a child, a whole slum starving in her eyes,
Within earshot of the Tuileries,
The French who are crazy or catholic enough
To place, facing each other, two tableaux
—One for the Men of the Convention, and one puffing
   the Orators of the Restoration—
At once made a circle wide as the sky around you
While the Mayor of the 5th *Arondissement*
Addressed the milling millions of Frenchmen:

"See how shapely small her adorable ass is;
Of what an incredible pink rotundity each cheek.
A bas Merovingian and Valois!
A bas Charlemagne and Henri Quatre!
For all the adulations we have paid them
In our fabulous *histoires*
They cannot raise an erection between them. Ah,
For too long has the madness of love
Been explained to us by sensualists and curés.
A bas Stendhal! *A bas* Bossuet!

"Forever and forever, from this blazing hour
All Paris radiates from Aviva's nest of hair
—Delicate hatchery of profound delights—
From her ever-to-be-adored Arche de Triomphe!
All the languors of history
Take on meaning clear as a wineglass or the belch of an angel
Only if thought of as rushing
On the wings of a rhinoceros towards this absorbing event.

Voyeurs, voyez! The moisture of her delicate instep
Is a pool of love
Into which sheathed in candy paper
Anaesthetized politicians drop from the skies!"
(Word jugglery of course, my Sweet; but the French love it
—Mistake it in fact for poetry.)

And the *applaudissements* and bravos
Bombinating along the Boulevard Saint-Germain
Made the poor docile Seine
Think our great Atlantic was upon it.
It overflowed with fright into the bookstalls
And sidewalk *cafés*.
Fifteen remaining *Allemands* with their cameras
Were flushed down the Rue Pigalle.

And when you were raised up
Into my hairy arms by the raving emotional crowds
Waving frenzied bottles of Beaujolais
And throwing the corks away ecstatically
(Not saving them!)
It was, my Love, my Darling,
As if someone had again ordered an advance
Upon the Bastille
Which we recalled joyously, face to face at last,
Had yielded after only a small token resistance.

Karen Connelly

Paris Is Not a Dream

1

Are there days?
Or only streets and paintings?
The catacombs of the city are mapped
        by calloused feet.
The heels of businessman
        peel from frenzied walking.
Do not offer your hand.
There will be a great rushing-in,
        a blur of feather, fur, fin.
Animals of all sorts feed here.

There are no leafy interiors,
        no weedy fields of crickets,
        no bouquets of hay and sky.
The parks stink of snapdragons and sex.
This is the Fine City, the Legend,
        any city, it seethes.
People live here, and die.
Their skin barely breathes.

Paris is not a dream
but a lie, a lace-at-the-throat duel,
a swordfight in red,
a shaken marionette
exquisite
and dead.

II

The old staircase swirls like a shell
        up to the soft centre,

the nest of raw silence that hides you.
You perch above the filthy sea of streets,
        feet cold on clay-stained tiles.
The bones in your toes crack when you rise.

The city bellows a famished roar.
You pick up the mouldy fists of bread from the floor,
        the little clumps of cheese,
        the broken wine glass:
                you hurl it all out to the gargoyles.
At night, you dream of trees
        but wake to a weed of sun in the sky.
Time pools quickly in the gutters under your eyes.

Each morning you journey underground,
        rake thrugh the pocked and perfect faces.
You search for the mask whose fissures
        are wide enough for your fingers.
But the Metro is tight and dry.
Her people fear your wet eyes.

Your face is round and bright,
        an innocent marble.

III

Men want to roll you back and forth
as you roll their names off your tongue.
Liqueurs and blue oysters slink down your throat.
so much hot bone draped with glinting skin
and fine cologne!
Jean-Louis, Jabar the Arab, Didier,
Dominique, Erik the mad Dane, etc.
Each cultured one an affectionate rapist.
Men stream and scatter like cockroaches.

Afterwards, you say to the neck
        of a man you cannot see:

I'm going for a walk now.
You rise; he does not open his eyes.
You take your walk like you take your tea,
        too quickly, gulping distance,
        burning your mouth on the acrid blackness.

Night wraps you up in a wet veil,
        sticks in your nose,
                stretches its purple tail
                        down your throat.

You sing under the bridges.
You watch rats eat old bread.
Half-drowned songs float in your head.
At night, the city is made of bricks, sewers,
                dregs of beautiful bodies,
                scraps of heart sinking in fountains.
Deep in St. Denis, bored prostitutes
        rinse their mouths of dirty rain.
Blue flesh bangs blue flesh, fiascos
        of neon creatures trapped by eyes.

Watching those bodies, you remember
        the men you've kissed,
        the tears pissed away in half-darkness
        beside foreign skin.
You clutch the little book in your fist,
        but your words are hiding.
The river pants like a dog on your face.
You remember your other country,
        but it is so far from this place.
the broken compass is wedged in your chest.
You neither run nor rest, but wait,
        your baffled eyes open wide.

IV

In the museums and churches,

like blades pass through your body,
lives waltz into your skeleton,
fingers press your eyelids

and the whisper of history is such
that you cannot hear your own blood.

Ghosts carry away pieces of your shadow in their mouths.
the lips of paintings brush your face.
there is blood in the oils, bones in the bronze,
        hearts churned into the walls,
        vast red bricks of memory.
The canvas is skin, the clay is meat.
Lives, stories, deaths, lives blaze silently around you,
        inhabiting your mind like a herd of fine-eyed horses.
You feel hooves pound against your cranium.

Christ is still pinned to our sin like a dragonfly.
In portraits that smell of spring, children
        are pressed shining among roses and dahlias.
You wander dazed through centuries,
        through fields of caught lives,
        mountains, deserts in Egypt—
                the gentle faces of camels
                turn to skulls before your eyes.

You plunge through midnight seascapes.
The moon's luminous hair sticks to your eyes
        at two in the afternoon.
Daggers from India are driven deep through your mind.
You trudge over frozen-fleshed snow,
        almost touch the frost-eaten fingers of soldiers.
The desolate light of these winters is so sharp
        your own eyelids stiffen with cold.

Pheasants and rabbits hand like brown tongues of silk.
their bodies slip over the edges of tables,
        mouths crimson with detail.

Vegetables around them are just ripe enough to eat,
        orange and green, and fruit swollen with juice.
Just under the warm canvas, the yellow apples are cool.

You want to strip your body of clothes, your mouth
        of tinsel words, you want to drop your twisted yarn
            of brain on the floor
            and plunge into the paintings,
            greet the cracked and open faces,
            faces like roasted chestnuts,
            warm and raw, eaten centuries ago,
                        but still here,

            lives, stories, deaths, lives
            more vibrant in paint than
            your own sweating fingers,
            faces, eyes, touching yours.

You feel hands in your hair, you hear the drunken songs,
        the weeping violins, the prayers of dying nuns,
        music mixed oil three hundred years ago.

In the empty galleries, there is a dazzle of windows,
        webs of glass entangling light.
The sun pierces with speckled body of day
        with golden claws.

That is what you want, everything:
            the old dream
            of drawing gold
          from the quick dust
            of moments.

In Versailles, the gilded horses are still,
        still rising
        gold out of the filthy water.

Daryl Hine

Le Rendezvous des Gourmets

The price is fixed, the courses foreordained,
Hors d'oeuvres, the soup of the day, unvarying vegetable;
Choice is limited to the inevitable
Crudities, what you call *delicatessen*,
The eternal hard-boiled egg...If you complain
The quality is always much the same,
Well, apart from physical pain and heartbreak
Our daily bread is dull, but it sustains us.

Then the main course, which tends to come too soon:
Steak or chicken, fried or boiled potatoes.
For those whom the doctor, disgust or conscience make
Vegetarian there is salad or plain noodles
And afterwards cheese, custard or an apple.
From egg to apple all has been too much,
Simple rations but in a tasteless profusion.
What one does twice a day if one is lucky.

What no one really likes to do alone,
Wine and love can make a celebration.
Thus every meal might be a sacrament
Once established, not only a last supper,
But a last breakfast, lunch and tea.
As often as one raised his glass or passed the mustard,
One might say—you or I might say, "As often
As you do this, do it in remembrance of me."

Steven Ross Smith

Pont Neuf on a Rainy Morning. 1931

(skin lifting
as i graze my tongue across her belly)

wet membrane
slicks curves of cobble-stones

wind-strokes ripple river's pellicle

he strides
in topcoat & fedora
dark against the sheening sidewalk
locked mid-step
between departing & arriving

something moves
a woman & a young girl
half gone
hurry at the edge
of his world

   (i cannot coax her back
   despite my longing)

behind, four human
shapes slip
in shade along
the further balustrade, ghostly
after-images
without names

   (i ache to hold her tightly
   in the growing
   & fading
   light)

Dancer. Centre Pompidou. 1988

shifting   in air   on stone

gestures   tight   as shadow's

scarce   body

in   black   moves

not   to   be   still   wind   whispers

crinkles   thin   blue   film   fingers

hold   fingers   pinch   space

within   without

brackets   a   syllable   of   air

courts   takes   in   lets   go

almond   eyes   closed   search

within   music   whose   metallic   melody   is

mood   &   tempo   though

impossible   blue   film   begins   to

cover   inch   by   inch

gesture   replaces   empty   space   in   wind

blown   blue   replaces   wind   in   blue

melts   into   cobble   grid   tucking

blue   beneath   curled   smallest

now   blue   tight   at   edges

tight   over   down-turned

head   hands   crossed

tiny   blessed   body

rocking   rocking   rocking

Chairs. Champs-Elysées. 1988

Avenue des Champs-Elysées Union de Banques a Paris Union de
Banques a Paris Change Change Cambio Wechsel AUDIO VIDEO
FLOPPY DISKS TDK COINTREAU Pakistan International PICON
PICON STYLOS PARKER Librairies BIRET SPECIALISTE DU
STYLO TAX FREE SOUVENIR DE PARIS DARRA CENTRAL
INTERIM saggel vendôme BUREAU A LOUER 950 M2 DIVISIBLE
RICHARD ELLIS BURTIN BRASSERIE DE L'ETOILE 33 Record dab
bier BRASSERIE DE L'ETOILE chair chair chair chair chair chair chair
RONSARD BOUTIQUE PIERRE CARDIN cinémas GEORGE V croc-
odile DUNDEE II Le monde entier l'adore Emmanuelle 6 Dirty
Dancing LE NOM DE LA ROSE UN PRINCE A NEW YORK CINE-
MA TOUS LES JOURS BALLY BALLY BALLY BALLY BALLY PIZZA
TUBORG BEER VUSUVIO BISTRO ITALIEN TUBORG BEER RIS-
TORANTE GRILL PIZZA VESUVIO TUBORG BEER VESUVIO
BISTRO ITALIEN TUBORG BEER chair chair chair chair chair chair
chair chair chair chair chair chair cinemas GEORGE V STALLONE
RAMBO III L'étudiante UNE AFFAIRE DE FEMMES Le vie est un
long fleuve tranquille Iraqi airways MAISON DU DANEMARK
RESTAURANT COPENHAGEN MAISON DU DANEMARK ROYAL
COPENHAGEN ROYAL COPENHAGEN COPENHAGUE RESTAU-
RANT FLORA DANICA RESTAURANT FIAT DELEGATION COM-
MERCIALE D'ITALIE FIAT Alitalia McDonald's McDonald's
McDonald's McDonald's McDonald's VOLVO MPS MONTE DE
PASCHI DI SIENA BANQUE FONDEE EN 1472 PEUGEOT TAL-
BOT 405 Flue voiture de l'année 1988 hutchinson hutchinson
BISTRO ROMAIN BISTRO ROMAIN BURGER KING BURGER
KING BURGER KING LE MENU DE LUXE A 20F AU LIEU DE
27.70F CAFE GEORGE V BRASSERIE RESTAURANT CAFE
GEORGE V BRASSERIE   chair chair chair chair chair chair chair
chair chair chair chair chair chair chair chair chair chair chair chair
chair LES FOURRURES MiLADY ACHETEZ AUJOURD'HUI AVEC
0F ET PAYER EN 89 LES FOURRURES MiLADY DUTY FREE
DETAXE A L'EXPORTATION MERCEDES-BENZ MERCEDES-
BENZ UGC NORMANDIE BIG TOM HANKS L'ART DE LA SECU-
RITE COGNAC CAMUS NAPOLEON NORMANDIE TOM HANKS
BIG BRUCE WILLIS PIEGE DE CRISTAL LA MAISON DE JADE
ROGER RABBIT LIDO OLYMPUS OLYMPUS PHOTO OLYMPUS
PHOTO OLYMPUS OLYMPUS OLYMPUS ENDOSCOPE OLYM-

PUS LUMINANCE MICROSCOPE OLYMPUS AUDIO TOSHIBA
VIDEO TOSHIBA COPIER JOKER JOKER JOKER jus de fruits
JOKER JOKER Audemars Piguet RIBOUREL Heyraud Heyrud
Heyraud Heyraud VERNET VERNET VERNET VERNET VERNET
VERNET QUICK ELYSEES RESTAURANT GRILL PATISSERIE BAR
CAFE QUICK ELYSEES GRILL KICKERS J.M. WESTON ROLEX
AIR AFRIQUE ROLEX CLARENCE ASSURANCES CENTRALES
DE FRANCE LEROY LEROY LEROY LEROY LEROY OPTIQUE
LEROY LEROY OPTICIEN THE FIRST NATIONAL BANK OF
BOSTON Elysées FIRST AVENUE PERFUMERIE PRET A PORTER
CLAUDE Champagne JACQUART Reims CHEMISE PLAY-BOY CRA-
VATE CHEMISE PLAY-BOY CRAVATE CHARTREUSE ELNASR
FRANCE TURQUIE ANDRE TURQUIE SERVICE D'INFORMA-
TION GODIVA CHOCOLATIER Maiffret STUDIO 102 discothèque
STUDIO 102 MONSIEUR ELYSEES MONSIEUR ELYSEES LINEA
DONNA MONSIEUR ELYSEES MONSIEUR ELYSSES MONSIEUR
ELYSEES MONSIEUR ELYSEES MONSIEUR ELYSEES piano bar
Cascades Elysees Tuborg Cocktails LUNCH CAFE SALON DE THE
chair chair chair chair chair chair chair chair chair chair chair chair
chair chair chair chair chair NATALYS NATALYS NATALYS LIGHT
LIGHT LIGHT LIGHT CREDIT SUISSE MANFIELD MANFIELD
Yves Rocher Yves Rocher LE TRIOMPHE DROWNING BY NUM-
BERS UN FILM DE PETER GREENAWAY demain c'était la guerre
un filme de YOURI KARA le HASARD 9 1/2 SEMAINES
BOUYGUES MAISON BOUYGUES point d'or LIBYAN ARAB AIR-
LINES OFFICE NATIONAL DE TOURISME DE THAILANDE
CLUB MEDITERRANE PANCALDI FRANCE CLUB MED CLUB
MED SKIEZ CLUB MED TOURISME EGYPTIEN CHARLES JOUR-
DAN CHARLES JOURDAN THE ECONOMIST CLUB PERNOD
LOWENBRAU MUNICH RESTAURANT BRASSERIE GALERIE
DES CHAMPS SOHO TAKE 5 2 NIVEAUX DE BOUTIQUES
NATIONAL BANK OF PAKISTAN BIMAN BANGLADESH AIR-
LINES TON SUR TON TON SUR TON TON SUR TON LA
BRIOCHE DOREE LA BRIOCHE DOREE BREL BREL fnac fnac
infinitifCABARET DES CHAMPS ELYSEES ARCADES DU LIDO 40
Boutiques dans une Galérie de Presitige Blanc Bleu Paris Blanc Bleu
Paris Blanc Bleu Paris Blanc Bleu Paris F. PINET F. PINET F. PINET
POINT SHOW LOISIRS CLARIDGE GALERIES du CLARIDGE
PIZZAZZ STALLONE RAMBO III MIDNIGHT RUN IRONWEED
MAX TISSUS MAX TISSUS Guerlain Guerlain Guerlain Lido

Musique Guerlain Guerlain FERINEL GROUPE PELEGE CAFE de
COLOMBIE GAUMONT CHAMPS ELYSEES Ce film est tiré du
roman de NIKOS KAZANTZAKI "Le Dernier tentation" il n'est pas
une adaption des évangiles MARTIN SCORCESE LA DERNIER
TENTATION DU CHRIST BRED POINT SHOW LINEA OMO
LINEA OMO PROCREDIT PROCREDIT PROCREDIT PROCRED-
IT PROCREDIT PROCREDIT PROCREDIT PROCREDIT PROCRE-
DIT PROCREDIT freetime freetime freetime freetime freetime free-
time freetime freetime freetime PRISUNIC PRISUNIC PRISUNIC
PRISUNIC VIRGIN MEGASTORE VIRGIN MEGASTORE VIRGIN
MEGASTORE SEIKO SEIKO virgin virgin virgin virgin virgin virgin
virgin virgin Ronyi PERFUMERIE VIRGIN MEGASTORE ON NE
FERA JAMAIS ASSES DE PLACE A LA MUSIQUE LOCATEL
LOCATION VIDEO GALERIE ELYSEES LA BOETIE DE VERLI DE
VERLI EDMOND EDMOND STULHER STULHER Groupe Pelloux
Groupe Pelloux Groupe Pelloux Groupe Pelloux Groupe Pelloux
Groupe Pelloux Groupe Pelloux Groupe Pelloux KELLY SERVICES
KELLY SERVICES KELLY SERVICES KELLY SERVICES KELLY SER-
VICES KELLY SERVICES KELLY SERVICES KELLY SERVICES
Gaumont Ambassade L'OURS P.E.L.L.E LE CONQUERANT BANK
TEJARAT CHANGE CHANGE Verlaine Verlaine Verlaine hamburger
Quick Restaurant Quick Quick LE COLISEE LE COLISEE chair chair
chair chair CITROEN HIPPO CITROEN GRILL RESTAURANT
GRILL HIPPO CITROEN BAR RESTAURANT HIPPO CITROEN
GRILL RESTAURANT Planar de Thomson Planar de Thomson Planar
de Thomson UN ZENITH POUR LE OUI UN ZENITH POUR LE
OUI UN ZENITH POUR LE OUI UN ZENITH POUR LE OUI UN
ZENITH POUR LE OUI UN ZENITH POUR LE OUI UN ZENITH
POUR LE OUI UN ZENITH POUR LE OUI RODIN RODIN
RODIN RODIN RODIN TISSUS RODIN TISSUS RODIN RODIN
MODE TISSUS LES PRIX LE MADRIGAL LE MADRIGAL chair
chair chair chair chair chair chair chair chair chair chair chair chair
chair chair chair chair chair chair chair chair chair chair chair chair
chair chair chair chair chair chair chair chair chair chair chair chair
chair chair chair chair INSTITUT PAB CITIBANK CITIBANK
CITIBANK COMPAGNIE GENERAL DE BANQUE CITIBANK
CHANGE ELYSEES 26 ELYSEES 26 ELYSEES 26 Galérie Elysées 26
Galéries Elysées 26 Galéries Elysées 26 Galérie Elysées 26 CAREL
GALERIE ELYSEES ROND POINT PARFUMS SILVERMOON
BEAUTE Avenue de Champs Elysées

George Elliott Clarke

Watercolour for Negro Expatriates in France

What are calendars to you?
And, indeed, what are atlases?
Time is cool jazz in Bretagne,
you, hidden in berets or eccentric scarves,
somewhere over the rainbow—
where you are tin-men requiring hearts,
lion-men demanding courage,
scarecrow-men needing minds all your own
after DuBois made blackness respectable.
Geography is brown girls in Paris
in the spring by the restless Seine
flowing like blood in chic, African colonies;
Josephine Baker on your bebop phonographs
in the lonely, brave, old rented rooms;
Gallic wines shocking you out of yourselves,
leaving you as abandoned
as obsolete locomotives whimpering Leadbelly blues
in lonesome Shantytown, U.S.A.

What are borders/frontiers to you?
In actual seven-league sandals,
you ride Monet's shimmering waterlilies—
in your street-artist imaginations—
across the sky darkened,
here and there, by Nazi shadows,
Krupp thunderclouds,
and, in other places, by Americans
who remind you
that you are niggers,
even if you have read Victor Hugo.
Night is winged Ethiopia in the distance,
rising on zeta beams of radio free Europe,
bringing you in for touchdown at Orleans;

or, it is strange, strychnine streetwalkers,
fleecing you for an authentic Negro poem
or rhythm and blues salutation.
This is your life—
lounging with Richard Wright in Matisse-green
parks, facing nightmares of contorted
lynchers every night. Every night.

Scatalogical ragtime reggae haunts the caverns
of *le métro*. You pick up English-language
newspapers and TIME magazines,
learn that this one was arrested,
that one assassinated;
fear waking—like Gregor Samsa—
in the hands of a mob;
lust for a black Constance Chatterley,
not even knowing that
all Black people not residing in Africa
are kidnap victims.
        After all, how can you be an expatriate
of a country that was
never yours?

        Pastel paintings on Paris pavement,
wall-posters Beardsley-styled:
you pause and admire them all;
and France entrances you
with its kaleidoscope cafés,
chain-smoking intelligentsia,
absinthe and pernod poets....
        Have you ever seen postcards
of Alabama or Auschwitz,
Mussolini or Mississippi?
        It is unsafe to wallow in Ulyssean dreams,
genetic theories, vignettes of Gertrude Stein,
Hemingway, other maudlin moderns,
while the godless globe
detonates its war-heart, loosing

goose-stepping geniuses
and dark, secret labs.

     Perhaps I suffer aphasia.
I know not how to talk to you.
I send you greetings from *Afrique*
and spirituals of catholic *Négritude*.
     Meanwhile, roses burst like red stars,
a flower explodes for a special sister.
You do not accept gravity in France
where everything floats on the premise
that the earth will rise to meet it
the next day;
where the Eiffel Tower bends over backwards
to insult the Statue of Liberty;
and a woman in the flesh of the moment
sprouts rainbow butterfly wings
and kisses a schizoid sculptor
lightly on his full, ruby lips;
and an argument is dropped over cocoa
by manic mulatto musicians
who hear the whispers of Eliot—
or Ellington—
in common prayers.

     You have heard Ma Rainey, Bessie Smith.
You need no passports.
Your ticket is an all-night room
facing the ivory, voodoo moon,
full of Henri Rousseau lions and natives;
and your senses, inexplicably
homing in on gorgeous Ethiopia,
while roman rumours of war
fly you home.

In Paris I Was Alive

Patricia Young
Untitled

I had always sensed Paris
in the back of my mind,
like a familiar road map
folded and refolded
so many times
the pieces had come apart
in my hands.
When I first arrived in Paris
it was like coming home,
or looking into my mother's face.
It was *deja vu*;
in Paris I was alive, confident,
tore along losing dresses,
cigarette cases, furs, hats and rings.
And if I ever saw something
of the *Real Paris,*
not the *America in Paris,* or
the *England in Paris,* but
the Paris that packed its bags
and headed for the countryside
when the tourists moved in,
it only left me hungry.

(Editor's note: this poem is in the voice of novelist Jean Rhys.)

F.R. Scott

Place de la Concorde

Love is a city
        loving is a thorough
                fare
      lovers are a populace
        each to each a crowded street
        so much happening
        and passing
    windows of wonder and colour where it is holy
        to stroll
    to discover
        doors domes the white façade
         intersections and little lanes

    O Arch of Triumph
    Notre Dame de Bon Voyage

The city of love sleeps
        hardly at all
      every road
     leads to the centre
    the traffic pours into a *rond point*
     turning slowly
    and it takes time
        to melt away

Three bells sound from a church
    lovers know it is a worshipping
    a holding aloft till
     it is finished
    and they are free to
      go

the city of love is
                        two cities
            divided by a river wide
                        as lovers are apart
            two banks
                        and walks by water
            different
            an element between

If the bridges stand
            if they are old and beautiful
            if underneath
                        there is the to and fro
            it is one life that is led
                        on both sides
            and only one name is given this city
      for it is always
                        a place
                                    of concord.

Stan Persky

Cocteau

He is in a vast field of white flowers. His name is Cocteau. A white horse is grazing under a cottonwood tree. He is writing something on white paper. A message.

Cocteau gets up & walks 17 paces to the East. In the middle of the field of white flowers he sees a porcelain shiny bathtub filled with blue water. The lovely white flowers are in the dirty boy's hair. The dirty boy has brown eyes & is washing his gangly legs. He is of course as always naked.

It is amazing.

Cocteau takes a long walk from where he is standing to the sea. He comes to his room. And goes in.

There is a flowerbox in the window. White flowers are growing there in a row. Cocteau takes out some paper & begins writing again. There is a boy sitting on the white bed scooping out chunks of red watermelon. He is getting the bed wet with the juice of the melon. Cocteau comes over & plucks a watermelon seed from where it is lodged in the boy's bellybutton. Cocteau is 24 & vastly amused. It is raining in Paris.

The rain falls for 7 years. Cocteau has a brown business suit on. Walking in the Parisian drizzle. Parisians don't mind it.

They are tolerant. Cocteau is wearing a white flower in the lapel of his suit. He is writing in a small notebook filled with white pages. Where is he going. He disappears into the white fog. He is gone. Gone. Where has Cocteau gone. Cocteau is like Coyote in English. There is a connection. Cocteau disappears in the fog at 31. Where will he reappear. We leave you in suspense.

Apollinaire

Apollinaire is in a chair outside the dentist's office. His teeth hurt. He is going to have a tooth pulled.

He is always seen in passing.

There are 4 chairs there. They are brown chairs. Apollinaire is waiting. Patient.

"God it hurts," he says.

In the other 3 chairs is Gertrude Stein singing her last golden opera to the hysterically giggling multitudes: Montparnasse cafe nocturne, Hummingbird smelling the Real Thing. And Modig. There are hundreds of reporters asking real questions.

Apollinaire's teeth are falling out.

"I think I'm going to be sick," he says. Who knows what he says.

They are sitting in 4 chairs outside the dentist's office waiting to have their teeth pulled out.

It suddenly is 4 chairs in a hall. Frenchmen are very excitable. On the whole likeable. Their passions are justified. They are throwing pineapples. & hissing—ssssss—snakes. The poets of the 1st French Poetry Renaissance are eating the pineapples. They are hungry. And haven't eaten for so long. Hungry.

The pineapples blow up into World War 1. Gertrude Stein bows. The audience giggles.

Apollinaire's mother is home cooking spaghetti in the hot kitchen. "Mmmm it's hot for july," she says, sadly.

Her son calls up. From Genoa. He got a contract. Yes, money. No, he is not dead. Yes, Italy mother. I don't know why. It required no thought he tells her. I wanted to. See Italy. Italy. Little me. Yes the lions are lovely here mother. O look the phone bill is piling up & I've got an appointment & they're signing the Armistice on a rowboat in the Marne & anyway mother I will send you a postcard—yes with a picture on it—it's the newest thing—picture postcards—I'm playing checkers with Mr. Pound, Chinese checkers—my pants fit—Italian tailors know what they're doing—goodby!

Louis Dudek

45

Love at all corners and songs
                    all night, all day
Yes, Paris is gay, as they say, nobody works
        everybody loves, whatever they do they do enjoy.
All morning the fruitstalls and markets stand open,
                    at 13 o'clock they close,
the little family sets up table
        in the place of affairs, takes bread and wine.
To sell they refuse, and it's impolite to disturb.
The waiters in the cafés try not to serve,
        you drink what you can get,
                        just sit and enjoy...
they say in the world there is despair,
        la crise, le déarroi (Gide and his boys,
                    and Sartre somewhere in the caves)
But the Parisians are gay, a city of clowns,
and though there's no special meaning to it all
                    —it's gay!

When you return home in Paris
                    at 24 o'clock
all the lovers in the street make way for you
as you ride, as they walk
                    along the street;
they open before you like a midnight flower
composed of lovers, every petal two
                    and in the middle of the flower,
                                        —you.

In the Place de la Concorde, where the guillotine stood
                    and did so much good
and did so much harm, we walked arm in arm
and got lost in the Louvre
                    that royal museum
with all those great bargains in art-books and cards.
King Louis in marble stood by then and smiled
                    at how we presumed
to look unimpressed by the size of his rooms
                    (so different the Renault from his coach-and-six,
different the traffic from tumbrils and sticks),
                    but in the Place
de la Concorde six days later
the familiar tables were turned
                    once more, & a broken bottle hissed
as the bullets shot by the police
                    hit or missed.
All to demonstrate...what?...(King Louis smiles)
—that there is still no peace, but a sword,
                    in the Place de la Concorde.

Andrew Wreggitt

Jardin du Luxembourg

The child is running when she sees you...leaning forward, she stumbles against the small gravel of the garden path, then sits, her face turned up towards us...We are resting, feet up, in metal chairs, autumn trees newly touched by frost, wide avenues of flowers under the criss cross of jet stream, toy sailboats in the fountain and the man near the gate cooking chestnuts, one eye scarred shut, an old song wavering under his breath and the warm smell of chestnuts as it rises, rises...

The small child sits in the gravel, two or three years old, looking at you, suddenly transfixed...as if it had all been about this moment from the beginning...these tiny marks from the soft shale pressed into the palms of her hands, her eyes so impossibly wide, running for sheer joy. "Allez, Marie." Her mother tugs at her arm, urging her up. But the child is stopped now and will not be moved, smiling at you, as if from a place inside her only she knows, this deep smile that is so like music it must...be music in fact...

...something even the tired mother hears for a moment, a little embarrassed, curious, following the child's gaze to your face. At this moment, all three of us looking at you...the smell of the chestnuts rising and the man who cooks them holding his wounded cheek in his cupped hand, the planes lifting and descending from Orly airport with such surety and ease, the sailboats in the fountain weathering each moment, pressing onward always...

..."Allez, Marie," the mother says more softly, amazed at the recognition in her child's face as she gazes at you, amazed as I always am...this recognition between all of us, all ways, as around us the smallest breeze moves past, bringing us the smell of chestnuts, touching the yellowed leaves with this one exquisite promise...

Cary Fagan

Giving

The drunk on the Rue de Buci who puts his too-firm arm around me
and tells me to enjoy life. (After I've refused his request for change.)
This is what I want to believe in: a city where the drunks are happy.

Couple

The Etruscan sarcophagus in the Louvre, of baked red clay. On the lid a sculpture of the married couple lying side by side, she in front and his arm around her, the two smiling as if they shared a secret.

In bed, we position our naked selves in just the same way. Our laughter suddenly turns solemn.

Radnóti

Miklós Radnóti, "drunk from writing poems," watched dawn rise over the city and listened to the cats mating on the roof. Paris, how many souls have loved you, but loved somewhere else more and so returned home again? Radnóti went back to Hungary to die in a mass grave, his pockets stuffed with poems.

But Miklós, that caressing sky above is your sky, so you must still be here...

J.M. Cameron

The Jews of Paris*

murdered

scattered

oppressed

In Paris all the bells
Break from the towers
In the violet morning

Sainte Geneviève Saint Denis
Saint Germain and
Notre Dame de Nazareth

Rue du Jourdain rue du Jourdain
You wind through the future's
Unimaginable vale

Bells reckon in consort
Rue du Jourdain rue du Jourdain
Le salut par les Juifs

Notre Dame de Nazareth
Turris Davidica
Turris eburnea

Temple Bellevile Place des Fêtes
I will share bread with you
Under the fictive wall.

I will break bread with you
Under that wall
As to your thirst

Vidi aquam
Egredientem de templo
a latere dextro

Alleluis & cetera
Rue du Jourdain rue du Jourdain
Rue des Rigoles

Rue de Belleville
Egredietem de templo
Eyes were gem-hard

Hearts chalk-dust
In forty and
Forty-one and

Forty-two and
Forty-three and
All along the

Rue de Palestine
Et la rue de Belleville
Egredientem de templo

a latere dextro
Alleluia & cetera

Rue des Rigoles

*With grateful thanks to Richard Cobb for "French Jews and Jewish Frenchmen," *Times Literary Supplement*, 10 October 1975.

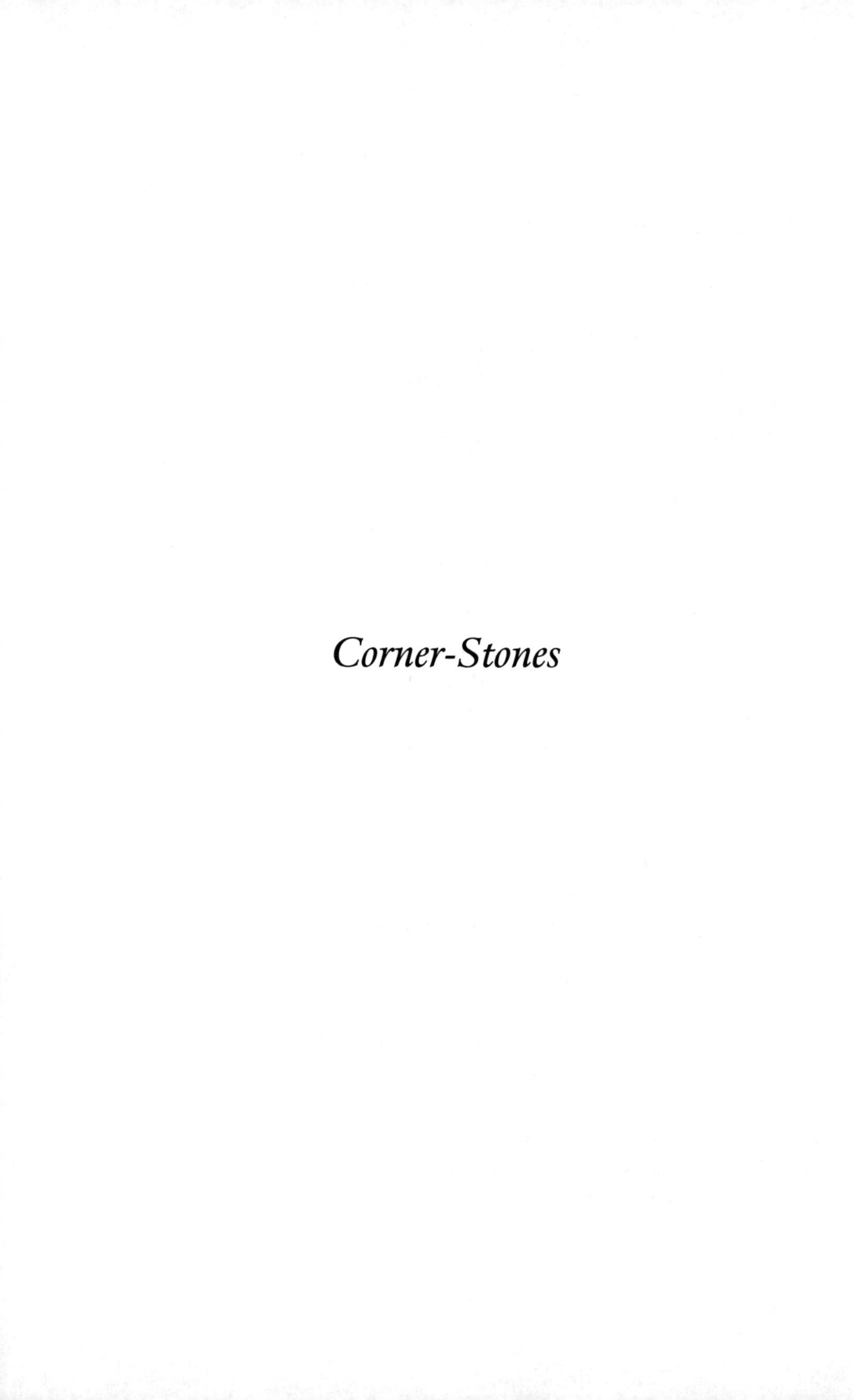

Corner-Stones

Dorothy Livesay
Old Trees at Pere la Chaise

Old trees drift silently all down the hill,
And stop beside the green grass at the gate.
Encaged with tombs, they feel the wind, and wait.

Beyond, the dust lies with a difference.
The crumpled dead lie huddled in these streets
Belleville and Memilmontant, Gambetta
The dead in cold damp tombs slip up and down
The stairs of bleak and shattered houses, grope
Into the bedroom, kitchen, lavabos in one—
Move there, and hate, and bring forth child
And then go creeping from the window's dust
Into the shrouded bed, the heavy sleep.
The sulking dead lie huddled in these sheets
Only to wake and stumble through the maze
The choking air of unenlightened streets.
What more can women do, so pitiful
With bundles of their own small flesh and bone
The wrinkled babies of the labourer
Than struggle from beneath the roots, the dust
Of Paris corner-stones and roofs, and crawl
With the old men, beside the jobless young
Up to the sunlight of the Cimitiere?
There, green grass growing in lush patches lies,
Shadows the stones; a little wind will play
Softly amid the canopy of trees.

The skulking dead lie huddled in these roots—
Old trees with spring wound round their head
And the sky's blue parasol above—
The crumpled dead, laden with urns and tombs
Slink downward from the sturdy, living roots
That clutch the earth for sweetness, to find there

The faded taste of dust, the choking air.
Old trees at Pere la Chaise that strive to rise
Above this stony city, carefully planned
A junk heap to immortalize
The body, since the shoul is shrunk—
Old trees, live longer! till a wilderness
Has covered stone and bone
And among the sunwarmed grasses
Eager children run!

Doves

Doves dive up and down
Across our window
Silver and shot amber.

Clouds drift
As snow drifts from hemlock
At a breath of wind.

If we lean out
From the window—
Paris
Irony of Eiffel
Tour Saint-Jacques
Sturdy Notre-Dame—
Under the smoke.

Preferable to imagine:
And to watch only, from within
Clouds, silver-spotted,
Doves, slow-circling,
Peace.

Bruce Meyer

Apollinaire

Nothing is dead but what has never been
The coloured past outshines tomorrow's grey
Besides whose formlessness it can display
The sequence of the effort and effect
                                        —'Cortège'

1

Let us say we went out in a little car
and returned at evening as the world changed—

the shades pulled low over the yellow glare
of lamps hung above evening meals, the estranged

deep blue of the east settling in for sleep
and the twilight coaxing old thoughts

from our tired brains. Suppose our escape
from the city this morning was a signal, that shots

rang out across distant borders, that words changed
and we became our guesses. Suppose you forgot

the subtleties of twilight and remembered the strange
darkness that gathered on familiar streets

and the faces of everyone you ever loved turned
to the earth you love, the half-rhymes complete

yet descending into the anarchy of whispers burned
into the silence until winter is no longer a symbol

but a companion who wants you dead. You
have an address, a place to stay and all

the words you can muster for a cry flow
through your fingers and grope along a wall.

This is the safe haven, you assume, this is
the true story pulled around you like a wish.

2

From what I remember of Paris I construct
the outlines of a scene, set in spring,

as chestnut blossoms open to conduct
a dialogue with the startled world, seeing

itself dragged into life again, pleading to be
poetry and needing someone to set it down.

And in the process, that street on which we
strolled arm in arm in search of our own

bread and candles becomes a shadow, the light
struggles at its edges and even the sound

of street bikes and distant music gathers dust.
In the process of telling a story and telling it right

the truth withers like red rose petals on the ground,
still red, still meaning rose, as if one must

convey that sense of something living, as if here,
in this poem, a line is drawn, the demarcation clear.

I shall preserve life at the cost of my own words
and they shall rise beyond the scene like startled birds.

3

Pretend we are not walking through ideas
but in a Paris street scene by Camille Pisarro.

As you sink into the activity, the avenues
flow off from one another down to narrow

points of reference and these you note in case
you should come this way again and the colours

are different. In a window above the rat race,
the one to the left of the dripping laundry floors

above the sidewalk, that's the one, we place
Guillaume Apollinaire who for several hours

has been redrafting 'Mirabeau Bridge,' the line
Les jours s'en vont je demeure taunting him

as he puffs his pipe hardpressed to define
the stationary wisdom that articulates the thin

line between one moment and the next. If ever
there was a cause to believe in poetry, if ever there

was a flicker of hope in the words themselves, never
had there been a moment to embrace it more. Where,

if the world of a word was without end, could
that end be confined, an echo floating like a raft

on the sea of obedience to the laws of time? The good
words, sighted, pass by like ships, and the draft

leaks water and limps along. O God of the wind
who inspires and wastes, this is not a painting nor

even a setting, but a struggle where there is no end
and I am a captain of truth longing for a native shore.

Douglas Fetherling

Harry's New York Bar in Paris

The bored waiter moves
towards you like a shark
in an aquarium
           turning quickly
when very close
having lived here many years
he knows the limits
and where the glass is
and is able to seem
calmly efficient
            while ignoring
the customers the dramaturges
who annoint themselves
              and mumble
amen into their drinks
to combat power withdrawal

What you think is the mood
is really the smell
           the threat
of posterity that keeps them
on their toes
        all the colours
have to be imported
nightly smoke is flown in
                special
like the noise
of the telephone ringing
with calls from persons long dead
and Jefferson's ghost
           playing
the piano

Don Domanski

Montparnasse

83

a small shadow
beneath my hand
the shadow of a late
afternoon in Paris
a thin damp skin
on the breeze
magpies lifting
their wingless god
into the air
Baudelaire's bones
like long pins
pointed down
into the earth

under him
a great ship
about to set sail
with a hundred
orphans
for a crew

all looking up
at the same moment
when their Mother
walks by
above them

down the Rue de la Gaité
down the Avenue de L'Ouest

on the surface of the earth.

Frank Davey

from "Dead in France"

The day I stumbled upon the tomb of Héloise & Abélard I wrote to
my friend Barrie describing the tomb & remarking on how many
different motives & desires had brought the pair to Paris & a
bourgeois graveyard, & the next month he is also dead. I had written
to Barrie because they were in the same graveyard as Gertrude Stein
& Apollinaire & the semiotics of these names all work differently from
out of the ground of a single graveyard. I was thinking of Barrie, & of
his thinking about the falling of saints into the words of people & of
what words Gertrude would have given to Abélard & Héloise.

*

Believing Abélard had not married Héloise & was refusing to marry
Héloise, her uncle hired assassins to kidnap him & cut off his balls.
Castration is a primitive method of birth control. The language of
violence here meets the languages of eros & logic. In some societies
castration has been used to enforce the paternity demands of others.
In *The Arabian Nights* eunuchs are expected to have recreational
intercourse, with the ladies of the harem. There is no record of how
"this barbarous act" *(The Encyclopedia of Philosophy)* affected the sexual
performance of Abélard. I like to imagine everyone in medieval France
believing that the sex life of him & Héloise was over & meanwhile
over & over they are enjoying what later would become fashionable as
"sex without fear."

*

The humanism of Abélard has been misread because of his
relationship with Héloise. Abélard held that sin does not reside in single acts but in the overall shape of a human life. I didn't ask Barrie
about the sex life of Héloise, I merely indicated I would send him a
copy of the text I was writing.

*

Various plot lines run through events. You & I are two of these plot
lines, & sometimes these plot lines become mysterious & sometimes
they appear to stop altogether. I went for a walk through a Paris
cemetery & along the way counted eleven well-fed cemetery cats. The

84

plot line of Canon Fulbert runs through the text life of Abélard &
Héloise. One fine morning by the Gregorian calendar. the day I left for
Paris, Barrie said he would miss me & I said I was going only for a
year & he replied sensibly that you never know what will happen in a
year.

*

Jim Morrison I now hear is also buried in Père-Lachaise although his
grave is not recorded in the official words of the tourist map. Crowds
are supposed to gather around it drinking & playing guitars & leaving
empty bottles & lunch bags on the adjacent graves, although the only
crowds I saw were five people at the grave of a Serbian nationalist, the
busloads walking to & fro the tomb of Héloise & Abélard & three cats
at their food dishes at the tomb of Marguerite Berthillon. A cemetery
is a complex proposition on ways & means for honouring the dead.

*

When Père-Lachaise was first opened early in the nineteenth
century Héloise & Abélard were moved here by the developers to give
panache to the new graveyard. What a shock to the bourgeois
sensibilities of Héloise's uncle was high-class stuff to the inheritors of
the Revolution. A cemetery is a complex proposition on how the dead
can enter the discourses of the living. Héloise had moved Abélard's
body to the convent of which she was abess shortly after his death in
1142, & was buried beside him when she died in 1164.

*

After Abélard's castration, both Héloise & Abélard joined religious
orders. In the fall that Barrie dies, the big cultural event in France is
the release of Nuytten's film *Camille Claudel*. Héloise named her son
Astrolabe, although there is no record that this helped her find her
way or even of where the son got to. Camille Claudel was the sister of
Paul Claudel, q.v. "Canon Fulbert made the unwilling Héloise become
a nun at Argenteuil." In the sixties, many unmarried California girls
named their kids Sky or Heavenly Love. "In shame," reports the
Encyclopedia Britannica, "Abélard embraced the religious life at St.
Denis." The cause of Abélard's shame is not specified, being
presumably self-evident. Abélard argued universals could reside in
things, which were necessarily unique. Héloise & Abélard had varied
ecclesiastical careers, which converged in 1129 when he founded the

85

convent of Paraclete with himself as abbott & her as abbess. He also argued that sin is not a substance or an act, but a consentment to evil. In the early 1130s he & Héloise composed a collection of their love letters & religious correspondence. At this point in the text the reader and writer can themselves compose erotic fantasies. Abélard came very close to arguing that all things & events, including sin, are composed of words, that universals are constructions of words, but as abbot of St. Gildas had poor relations with his monks & was nearly murdered.

*

I've checked my map & there seems to have been no grave in Pére-Lachaise marked "August Rodin." Rodin, Nuytten's film suggests, is the sentimental & melodramatic French sculptor who stole the heart and best ideas of his girl pupil & became, like Abélard, acclaimed as a genius. If you stroll the graveyards of France, you can detect many of the master narratives of French culture. Have we been missing something, Barrie, about our students? Freud owes a prodigious debt to his hysterics. *Dead* seems a reasonable adjective to modify Héloise or Abélard or Auguste Rodin but is painful to place in front of the name of a close friend. For this reason the movie-goers weep incredulously as Camille is locked away into thirty years of dying by her mother & brother.

*

My daughter observes that all the film reviewers write of Rodin & Camille & not Auguste & Camille or Claudel & Rodin & certainly not Auguste & Claudel. I reply that maybe they read *Claudel* as a previously assigned signifier. She does not look satisfied. Rodin gets a two-column entry in most encyclopedias but Claudel gets none except in the *Britannica* where the full entry reads "Rodin's mistress and model." This story of my trip to a graveyard doesn't look like any poem or novel I've read. Maybe it shows too much concern with death or too much fascination with the seduction of talented young women. Although Barrie didn't get to the Tarascon festival, feeling too ill to travel, the rest of the Horsemen did, & one of them, Paul Dutton, came to my little apartment two blocks from the cemetery. Camille & Abélard as victims of phallocratic justice. My son opened a bottle of Bordeaux. Héloise & Camille as victims of phallic inscription. No, said Paul, I think I prefer to remember Gertrude as someone living.

86

Robert Finch

Eiffelwise

Fans who mount the Tour Eiffel
Know what they are doing well,
Care not architects have sniffed
At Gustave Eiffel's tall success
And hasten upward in a lift
To what for them spells happiness—
The *downward* trip. No neophyte
Can see (till he has tried) they're right.
The real *tour de la tour's* on foot
Or not at all; your tower-fan
Par excellence an Eiffelman,
Alone can adequately put
Meaning in 'esprit d'escalier':
The downward way's the only way
To know the tower and its *mystique*.
Twelve flights of stairs comprise the trick,
Six long, six short, make up the quorum
Of Eiffel's *scala asinorum*.
Down, down, down, into the lattice
Of the strangest tower that is,
Enormous ingenuity,
Ingenious enormity.
Descending this unique giraffe
To the first landing makes one laugh
But there one turns and turning quails
For now its short leg drops, one fails
To see a thing except a dive
Far to the Champ de Mars below
Which, *that* way, none has reached alive!
From here the going's more than slow,
The flights seem steeper and the ground
Looks farther at each downward round.
Dazed in this race of space one spies
No vertical in all the splay,
No horizontal helps the eyes,
The stair is a diagonal

With no right-angle joints at all,
Even the horizon loses face
Through such oblique metallic lace,
This caged, in-caving cavity
That is not held by gravity
Nor yet, like Gothic or Baroque,
Coheres by weight of rock on rock
But clings together through the tensile
Strength of its members and the shear
Pull of its bolts, a weight prehensile,
Wrapping itself round the air,
Pitting itself against the wind
Which blows in front, around, behind,
And, as its crucial loading, must
Thrust high what's hooked into earth's crust,
Not founded on it, antithetic
To every law at all aesthetic.
Eiffel is no Vitruvius, nay,
Nor yet a Le Corbusier,
Building with Euclidean grace.
Eiffel's a pioneer in space,
The space of space-ships that rely
On no external force to guy
Their structural coherency.
Never forget that this was done
Before our century had begun.
Back in 1889,
The brain-child of a solid, fine
And portly bourgeois of unshakable
Probity, an unmistakable
Model patermailias he,
With beard, top hat,
Collar, cravat,
And every last accessory,
Inside of which there was a mind
Of mood serenely disciplined
Yet from convention so unchained
That still it signals from his tower
to all who tremble at this hour:
No intellectual freedom bears
Relationship to what one wears.

Organ-Recital, Notre-Dame-de-Paris

Where down the middle ages ever stirs
A Multitude like this? Long skirts and shorts,
Long hair and none; cowls, capes, shawls, shirts
That dangle from blue jeans, hippies in furs,
Bourgeois in collars and ties, tourists with macs,
Music-lovers, curiosity-seekers, shy
People who come to pray and stay to try,
Children bewildered in their parents' tracks,
No seats, no standing-room. A pale cold sun
Stares through stained glass at muted expectation.
The organ shudders with improvisation
As heterogeneous as the crowd. Not one
Budges. Then pandemonium. At the doors
Sisters tend bowls that the stampede ignores.

Janet Read

Parisian Courtyard

midi

sun plunges like an elevator
ten stories into the courtyard
noon white obelisk

goldfish journey in a small pond
radiant flames in green cloisters
light climbs to a square blue sky

gold discs scatter across the Seine
as St. Germain pierces the sun

quatre heures de l'après midi

tea is a still life
rooted to white ironwork
tables, chairs are arabesques

sun creeps up the wall
slides away
you understand the oubliette's
grey descent, desolation

in strange buildings
spirals under your eyelids.

following the sun
gulls are tattered papers,
kites dancing.

two blocks away
a Jewish restaurant explodes

frontiers, battle lines;
you draw the mind's Maginot line
reject violence, generate

nostalgia for white villages
under green summer leaves, Ontario

corn stands, rifles in the field.

six heures

evening white birds circle
singing towers, courtyards
where newspapers curl
sleepy snails on tables

high up, blue opens
to pink bellied clouds

sun fades sky, drops
over the world's edge

vapour whispers above the river
goldfish dangle in liquid sleep.

Paris, Rue des Pères Saintes, 1980

Stephen Scobie

Metro

I always carry in my wallet an unused ticket for the Paris Métro; it takes me through the turnstiles of return.

You will think perhaps of the Guimard entrances, of their curved carved metal growing like leaves, the arabesque of the 1890s as it arches over the stairways that lead you down. Down into that subterranean maze (the crossing corridors of Chatelet), the phantom map of the second city, underground.

Line 4 on the current system, Chapelle to Clignancourt, was in the 1920s called *Nord-Sud*. Pierre Reverdy took that name for his magazine, trying to link the artistic communities of Montmartre and Montparnasse, the old and new Bohemias. It runs, still, through the heart of the city: Cité, St Michel, Odéon....

And then there are dead sttions of the Métro (croix Rouge, for example): closed down, abandoned, the exits boarded up, the shabby platforms glimpsed in the dark as the trains rattle through. Ghost places, hollow names—

—"the apparition of these faces in the crowd."

Return.

CONTRIBUTORS

J. M. Cameron was born in Manchester, U.K. in 1910. A professor in England for many years, he came to St. Michael's College of the University of Toronto in 1971. Among his books is a collection of poetry, *The Music Is in the Sadness (1988)*.

Bliss Carman(1861-1929) was born in Fredericton. He attended the University of New Brunswick and worked for a time as a literary journalist in New York. Author of over fifty books of poetry, he is best known for his regional poems of the east coast. He was awarded the Lorne Pierce Medal for distinguished service to literature. He died after a reading tour.

George Elliott Clarke hails from the Black Loyalist community of Three Mile Plains, Nova Scotia. He is the author of three books of poetry, including *Lush Dreams, Blue Exile* (1994). Currently he is a professor of English and Canadian Studies at Duke University, Durham, North Carolina.

Karen Connelly was born in Calgary in 1969. She is the author of three books of poetry and a memoir of living in Thailand, *Touch the Dragon*, which won a Governor General's Award.

Frank Davey was a founder of the literary journal *TISH* in the early 1960s. A professor at York University in Toronto, he has published books of poetry, criticism, and cultural studies. The full text of "Dead In France" can be found in his collection of prose poems, *Popular Narratives* (1991).

Don Domanski was born and raised on Cape Breton Island; he lives in Halifax. His books include *Wolf-Ladder* (1992) and *Stations of the Left Hand* (1994).

David Donnell won the Governor General's Award for poetry in 1983 for *Settlements,* from which his two poems are taken. His most recent book is *China Blues*. He has never been to Paris.

Louis Dudek was born in Montreal in 1918 and taught literature at McGill University, retiring in 1982. The first edition of *Europe* (including the poems reprinted here), was published in 1955 by Contact Press. It was published in a new edition by The Porcupine's Quill in 1991.

Cary Fagan is most recently the author of *The Animals' Waltz* (1994), a novel. The work included here is taken from *The Little Black Dress: Tales from France* (1993).

Douglas Fetherling is a poet and visual artist whose books include *Travels By Night: A Memoir of the Sixties,* and *Selected Poems,* both published in 1994.

Robert Finch was born on Long Island in 1900. He studied at the Sorbonne in Paris before joining the University of Toronto's department of French. About his poem "Eiffelwise" he writes: "For some years I lived with a view of the Eiffel Tower from my room and came to know it in all its moods as well as often visiting its extraordinary anatomy."

C.H. Gervais is an award-winning journalist at *The Windsor Star* as well as the author of many volumes of poetry. In 1994 he published a book of poems, *Playing God,* and a collection of interviews with major religious figures.

John Glassco (1909-1981) left for France in 1928 and returned to Canada three years later, eventually settling in the Eastern Townships of Quebec. He produced poetry, fiction, translations of French Canadian poetry, and his celebrated *Memoirs of Montparnasse* (1970).

Ralph Gustafson (1909-1995) lived for a time in England and New York before returning to the Eastern Townships of Quebec, where he was born. His many honours included the Governor General's Award for Poetry and the Order of Canada. His *Collected Poems* have been published in three volumes.

Daryl Hine was born in Vancouver in 1936 and has lived in the United States since 1967 where most of his books have been published. A Canada Council Award in 1958 allowed him to live and study in France for several years.

Judith Krause lives in Regina. She is the author of two books of poetry, *What We Bring Home* (1986) and *Half the Sky* (1994).

Irving Layton, one of Canada's best-known and most controversial poets, arrived in Montreal from Romania at the age of one. His books include *A Red Carpet for the Sun* (winner of the Governor General's Award in 1959), and *A Wild Peculiar Joy* (1982).

Dorothy Livesay was born in Winnipeg in 1909 and published her first book of poems at the age of 18. She has combined poetry writing, political activism, and teaching. Her poems published here can be found in her collection of essays and reminiscences, *Right Hand Left Hand* (1977). She lives in Victoria.

Bruce Meyer is the author of two collections of poetry: *The Open Room* (1989) and *Radio Silence* (1992). He teaches literature in the School of Continuing Studies at the University of Toronto.

Stan Persky travelled in Europe with the U.S. Navy in the late fifties and early sixties and lived in San Francisco before moving to Vancouver. He teaches philosophy at Capilano College and is the author of *Wrestling The Angel* (1977), *Buddy's* (1991), and other books.

Janet Read is a poet and artist whose work has been shown in solo and group exhibitions across Ontario. Her first book of poetry, *Blue Mind's Flower*, was published in 1992. She lives in Port Hope, Ontario.

Stephen Scobie was born in Scotland and has lived in Canada since 1965. *McAlmon's Chinese Opera*, from which the poems here are taken, won the Governor General's Award in 1980. Scobie has lived in Paris for extended periods in 1975-6 and 1985 and "continues to visit the city obsessively." He reports that his favourite café is the Bonaparte, on the rue Guillaume Apollinaire.

F.R. Scott (1899-1985) was the dean of law at McGill University from 1961 to 1964. His work both as a translator of French Canadian poetry and as a social philosopher earned him Governor General's Awards. He also received the award for *The Collected Poems of F.R. Scott* (1981).

Robert Service (1874-1958) came to Canada from Scotland in 1896. His first collection of verse, *Songs of a Sourdough* (1907), became enormously successful and he eventually gave up a banking career to continue writing popular ballads and novels.

Steven Ross Smith lives in Saskatoon. His work here is taken from *Transient Light* (1990), a book consisting of parallel sets of poems describing Toronto and Paris. "Pont Neuf on a Rainy Morning. 1931" is based on a photograph by André Kertész.

Phyllis Webb was born in Victoria in 1927. She has lived in England, Paris, San Francisco, and Toronto, and currently resides on Salt Spring Island, B.C. "A Walk by the Seine" was published in her book *Even Your Right Eye* (1956). A Governor General's Award recipient, her most recent work is *Hanging Fire* (1990).

Andrew Wreggitt of Calgary is a poet, playwright, and screenwriter. He has won first prize in the CBC Literary Competition for poetry and the Alberta Writers' Guild Stephan Stephanson Award for *Making Movies* (1989).

Patricia Young was born in 1954. Her poetry has earned her the Pat Lowther Memorial Award and the British Columbia Book Prize. *All I Ever Needed Was a Beautiful Room*, a poetic sequence on Jean Rhys, was published in 1987.